RAPID READING

Janis Grummitt

illustrator: Roger Keys

THE INDUSTRIAL SOCIETY

Contents

Foreword

1 Introduction 1
Objective 1
Misconceptions 1

2 What is reading? 2
When is reading not reading? 2
How can we not read aloud? 3
Reading a positive act 4
Attitude 4
The skills of reading 4
Poetry and novels 6
Summary 6

3 Speeding up 7
How fast do you read? 7
Eye movement 8
Fixations 8
Action to improve fixation 9
Regression and visual wandering 10
Reading faster—mental barriers 11
Physical problems 13
Summary 13

4 The right approach 14
Flexibility 14
What approach? 14
The gears 14
What factors affect the style of reading? 15
Combinations of gears 20
Summary 20

5 Understanding and remembering 21
Understanding 21
Rules for being critical 22
Memory 23
Retention 24
Recall 25
Association 25
Labelling 26
Summary 27

6	**Skimming**	28
	Scanning and sampling	28
	Locating	29
	Summary	30
7	**Studying**	31
	Summary	31
8	**Final Summary**	32
Appendix 1	**Reading tests**	34
Appendix 2	**Marking chart**	39
Appendix 3	**Reading speed conversion table**	40
Appendix 4	**Answers to reading tests**	42
Appendix 5	**How to test yourself**	43
Appendix 6	**Further reading**	44
Appendix 7	**Industrial Society courses**	

Foreword

A manager is distinguished from other employees by the fact that she/he is responsible for getting work done by the people who report to her/him. In an era when systems for transmitting information have been developed to an amazing standard of speed and volume this key responsibility can be hindered by the substantial but necessary administrative workload.

Many managers complain about the 'mountain of paper' that they have to deal with. The manager can possibly deal with this by more effective planning of time and by adopting a systematic approach to delegation. However, if this still leaves a great deal of written material to digest then it will be of great value to him or her to be able to dispose of that material as rapidly as possible.

Janis Grummitt's book provides some simple guidelines for rapid reading without loss of understanding and retention. It is based on the experience of many managers, particularly the hundreds who have attended the *Rapid reading* course run by The Industrial Society. It should prove a very effective aid for the increasingly busy manager.

YVONNE BENNION
Division Director

1 Introduction

Objective

The object of this book is to help the reader towards a more efficient method of reading and to point out a few bad habits which may be slowing the reader down. As a result of practising on the lines suggested in this book, the reader will be able both to increase his speed of reading and improve the quality of his comprehension and retention. It is important to recognise that the right approach to reading is as important as reading 'rapidly'. It is efficiency we should aim at, and not the sort of misconceptions mentioned below.

Misconceptions

1   *The magic wand theory*
People often ask the inevitable question: '. . . quickly, can you tell me what the secret to speed reading is?' Many people assume that a book or a course on rapid reading will act rather like a fairy godmother's magic wand passing over them . . . that they will automatically become speed readers once they know what the 'gimmick' is. There is no 'secret' formula, there are no 'gimmicks': there is merely a great deal of practising with the right attitude. The reason that results often appear spectacular after a course of personal practice is that most of us read with the wrong approach and develop bad habits as we grow up; once these are eliminated actual speed is obviously increased.

2   *The 'faster-than-light' reader*
Another common fallacy is that after learning the techniques and doing some practice, one could easily read the whole of the *Sunday Times* in five minutes during breakfast, or get through the complete works of Shakespeare on the train going to work. It cannot be done, at least not if you want to take in anything you are reading. No course or book will enable you to achieve these amazing feats, only an act of God will do this!

This book contains good practical advice. It will improve reading ability very greatly if:

- a new attitude to reading is adopted
- the techniques and suggestions in the book are adhered to
- the reader practises this new approach regularly.

First, we need to start by rethinking our attitude to reading. The following chapter should start you off with a new approach.

2 What is reading?

Think back to school days. How did you learn to read? Most of us went through the process of taking our *Red Reader* out to the teacher and pronouncing the words to her one by one. Obviously, as time passed, we began to 'read in our heads'. Most of us continued to read by pronouncing all the words—only silently to ourselves. Most people continue reading in this manner for the rest of their lives—assuming that reading aloud and reading silently are the same thing, only one is quieter! This is where the canker sets in. The wrong attitude towards reading has been developed. Failure to teach children how to read 'in their heads' as a separate technique results in a population of inefficient readers. *We do not need to pronounce to be able to understand our reading.* Let us examine why.

When is reading not reading?

Reading aloud is a slow process and so is 'reading aloud' in our heads, or 'subvocalising'. It is slow because it involves the recognition of the word, then the pronunciation of that word, and then the interpretation of it in the context of the passage. The interpretation of the word is vital, or the exercise ceases to be 'reading', it merely becomes a recognition exercise. So we can be 'reading' aloud and not reading at all. Consider, for example, a French text. We have a knowledge of French pronunciation and a few French words, but a poor ability to translate into English. It is possible for us to read the French passage aloud very competently, but we would not have understood a single word in it. So was this really reading? Another example of this, which may be more familiar, is the case of the tired reader. The tired person can 'read' a whole page of a book, but realise after doing so that he has understood and taken in absolutely nothing. He may go back and pronounce all the words again, but he still may not have read a thing.

This illustrates the point . . . that there are two major parts to reading:

- recognising
- interpreting.

Pronouncing the word does not ensure that we have understood it. We do not have to pronounce in order to recognise and interpret. It is essential for the oral presentation, but unnecessary for the personal reading exercise.

How can we not read aloud?

A major fear is that we will not be able to understand if we do not 'say it', but we can make the reading process far more efficient when reading silently if we miss out the unnecessary stage of pronunciation. When reading aloud our intention is to communicate the written material orally to someone else. When we read silently there is no need to do this at all.

Words are symbols. In our language we can express these symbols in two different ways: graphically as on paper or orally as sounds. Sound symbols are for oral communication, written graphic symbols are for the equivalent communication to a reader. The confusion arises where the two uses of a symbol are used together. At school, reading is taught as an oral exercise and so the graphic symbol and the sound symbol are automatically assumed to be used together. This is not the case. When using a sound symbol (word) it is not necessary to be shown also the graphic representation of that sound to be able to understand it. Why is it then, that we assume the opposite is true, ie that in order to understand the written word we need to be able to hear the associated sound?

So we should have a situation like this in both cases:

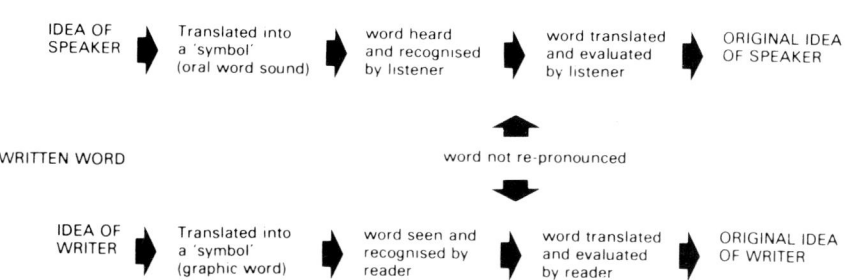

Take an example of a situation where we do automatically follow the above example, where we have a visual symbol, but never pronounce it before interpreting. If we see a road sign while driving like this one

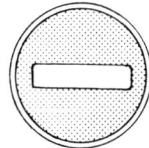

we do not pronounce it to ourselves by saying 'a red sign with a white line through the middle' or 'no through road'. We recognise the sign and interpret it automatically. A good reader does exactly this with the written word. However, we have been taught to read by pronouncing—so you will quite naturally continue to 'subvocalise' until you are reading too fast to do so. Do not try to stop—you will find this very difficult; rather concentrate on reading faster and *do not worry* if you are not pronouncing sometimes.

Reading a positive act

It is possible, after the comparison we have just made between the spoken and written word, to refer to reading as a sort of 'listening with the eyes'. Unfortunately, another idea that most of us seem to develop at school is that both reading and listening are negative reactions. So, if we are making a speech, or writing an article, we must be making an effort, putting a lot of energy in to the action. If we are listening to the speech or reading the article, however, it is generally felt that there is very little effort involved. So we tend to say: 'I was just reading, that's all.' Reading is thought to be a passive activity, one looks at the page and the author has done all the work. This is not true. An efficient reader, like a good listener, is putting just as much effort into his part of the communication as the writer or speaker did originally. If there is no hard work (as in the case of our sleepy reader), then there will be no understanding. Reading is a skill and a positive action which requires a great deal of effort.

Attitude

So reading is not quite as easy as it seemed at school. Quite a number of skills have to be developed in order for us to become really expert readers. It is these skills that you will learn from this book. However, old habits die hard, and unless the basic change of approach is made at the start, there will be very little improvement. A lot of barriers will have to be broken down, the biggest one being the pronunciation barrier—the ability to see words as symbols representing the writer's ideas rather than as individual items with intrinsic meanings. Having the right approach to reading is half the battle of becoming more efficient.

The skills of reading

What are these skills that we have to develop? Let us relate them logically to the reading process itself. Opposite is a diagram outlining the basic reading process.

This may appear to be a very complicated and lengthy procedure, but in fact the mind in reality performs each one of these stages almost simultaneously. Perhaps we have just come up against our second major barrier—that of fearing the limitations

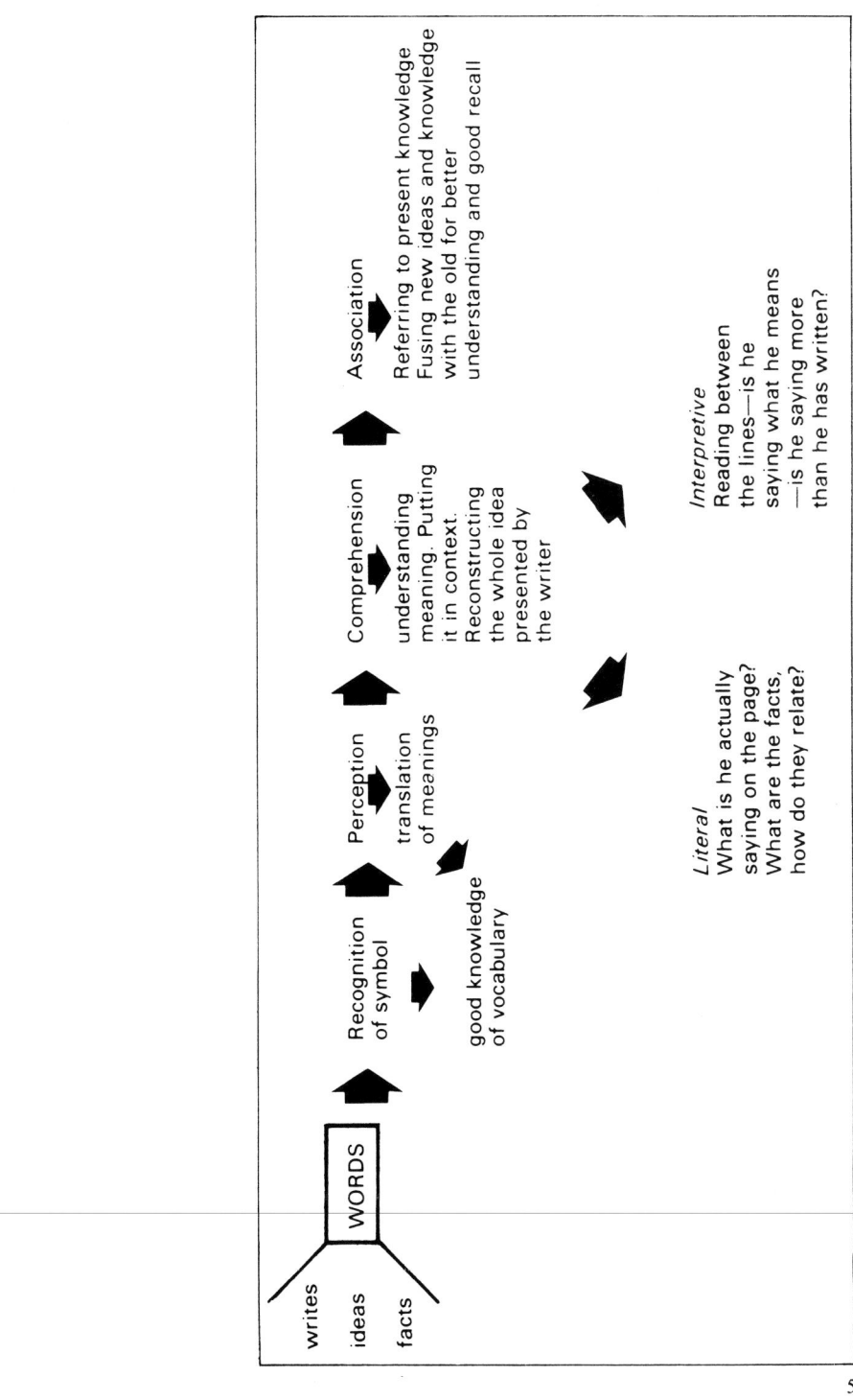

of our brain. Apart from the obvious limitations of vocabulary in some cases, intelligence bears no relation to reading ability. The exception to this may be the person of below average intelligence. Provided that one is above average intelligence, then a person with an IQ of 120 is likely to be just as good a reader as the person with an IQ of 180 (maybe even better). Our brains are capable of far more than we imagine, and it is unfortunate that most of us grossly underutilise our minds in everyday life. To read efficiently, we need to use them to their fullest extent, and not underestimate their capabilities.

Poetry and novels

It must be emphasised for those lovers of literacy among us, that it is not always desirable to miss out the pronunciation stage in reading. The enjoyment of a work of art is often in the sound of the words themselves and how they are expressed. This is especially true in poetry. In these cases it is necessary to be able to switch from the type of reading described in this chapter to the original 'pronunciation' method. This is all part of the flexibility needed by a good reader.

Summary

This chapter has drawn the basic distinction between reading aloud—pronouncing the symbols—and reading 'in our heads' without the pronunciation. Thus reading must involve interpretation as well as recognition. This will require a significant change of attitude to reading, and a positive approach.

1   You need not worry about 'saying' each word
2   You must treat reading 'positively'
3   You will not improve without adopting this new attitude
4   You must not allow fears of your own limitations stop you from improving
5   You must not attempt to use this approach on literature you read for pleasure.

3 Speeding up

The last chapter dealt with the problem of understanding the thought processes necessary for efficient reading. There are, however, after we have grasped this essential background thought, several points we can examine from a purely physical point of view. As most of our training in reading finished at the recognition stage, few of us develop independently towards advanced reading and many of us become lazy in our reading habits, so that an average person on average material will read at around 250 words per minute (that is about a foolscap page of longhand writing). This is too slow. The many rapid reading courses that have developed in recent years attempt to help the reader to adopt new habits and develop a much faster style of reading. It must be pointed out, however, that as we get older many of us suffer from recognition problems due to poor eyesight —have your eyes tested regularly.

How fast do you read? It is very difficult to assess reading speed without having any guidelines.

Exercise In order to find out whether you are a fast or slow or average reader, turn to appendix 1 and do a reading test before going any further.

The exercise you have just completed also tested comprehension of the material. This is most important because it is one thing to read at 600 words per minute and have a good understanding of a passage, and to read at 600 words per minute and not know the first thing about it. The speed of reading must always be considered in conjunction with the understanding of what has been read. On material of this difficulty an average reader would expect to get between 60 and 70 per cent comprehension with a speed of about 250 words per minute. This may act as a rough guide to your own present ability.

Some people naturally read more quickly than others. This is not related to intelligence or, as far as we know any other such factor, age, sex (although many men complain that their wives are amazingly fast). It must, therefore, be related to the technique employed in reading.

Eye movement   Let us look at the physical factors involved in reading How do our eyes move? Most people, asked this question, would reply that the eyes move smoothly across the page from left to right along each line and back again, as in the diagram here:

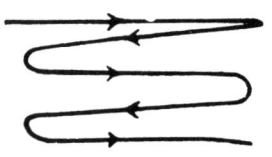
How most readers think their eyes move

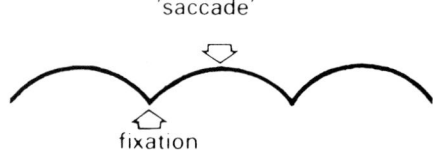
How the eyes actually move

This is not the case, however. In 1890 a French ophthalmologist called Emile Javal, disproved this theory by testing peoples' eye movements as they read. He discovered that eyes do not move smoothly at all. In fact they 'jump' from one focus to the next. Javal termed the 'jumps' as 'saccades' and the focusses as 'fixations'. From this discovery other interesting points were noticed. A fundamental difference could be traced between the fast and the slow reader by monitoring these eye movements. The same passage was read more efficiently by one reader than the other. The following examples will illustrate the differences noticed.

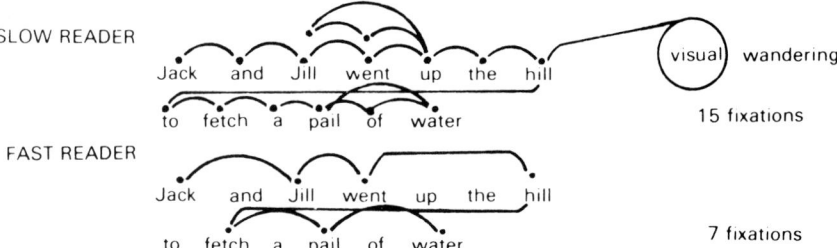

It should be noticed that there are two major differences here.
- the slow reader fixes on every word
- the slow reader goes back, 'regresses', to re-read certain words, as well as wandering at times.

Fixations   So a critical factor in faster reading is the number of fixations.
Obviously, this is not the only problem, for the length of time taken for each fixation is also important.

The time taken for each focus can vary between 1/5 second and 1½ seconds. Some readers would obviously benefit from attempting to quicken this time to be nearer the 1/5 second minimum. This is perfectly possible for us, as the brain can register as many as five words in 1/100 second. It is a question of accepting that we are merely *recognising* the words in order to interpret them and *not* attempting to pronounce them—this will slow up fixation time *and* prevent us from breaking the 'reading-every-word' habit.

Let us examine what sort of a difference these two points make. Taking the number of fixations alone:

    the slow reader makes 15 fixations

    the fast reader makes 7 fixations.

If we assume, for the sake of this argument, that they both have an average fixation time of 1 second, then our slow reader takes 15 seconds and our fast reader takes 7 seconds to read the same material. Magnify this by a whole page and then an entire book and the difference becomes very significant. If it takes the fast reader a week to read a book, it takes our slow reader at least two weeks! In terms of a year's reading of books, this means that one gets through 52 books in a year, while the other will get through only about 25.

Let us look at fixation time next. Again, if we assume that both our slow and our fast reader make 7 fixations, if one fixes for 1½ seconds and the other for 1/5 second, then it takes this long:

    the slow reader takes 10½ seconds

    the fast reader takes 1 2/5 seconds.

Putting both of these results together we see that the difference between our slow reader (too many fixations and too long) and our fast reader (a fewer number of shorter fixations) is:

    the slow reader takes 15 fixations of 1½ seconds
                    = 22½ seconds

    the fast reader takes 7 fixations of 1/5 second
                    = 1 2/5 seconds

Now the difference is considerable!

Action to improve fixation

1   *Cut down the length of each fixation.* This means trying to read faster; not lingering over words; pushing yourself faster all the time. Read another passage and time yourself. It is possible to increase reading speed by 25 per cent by merely willing to do it. Regular tests to monitor speed are very useful to check that speed continues to increase. You should always aim to increase

9

on every exercise. It is only practice that will make a significant improvement here. See appendix 5 for details on how to test yourself at home or at work.

2   *Stop fixing on every word.* This does not mean skipping words—yes you do *READ* every word, but do not fix on every one. It is very easy to look at one word and see the two words on either side simultaneously. Try it. Fix your eyes on the middle word below and take in the other words without looking at them specifically.

The cat sat.

Always try to fix on verbs or nouns. That is, the words that describe what is being done, or what the facts are. Words such as 'and', 'but', 'when' are so common and easy to recognise that they can be taken in along with a fix on a more significant word. This does not mean these words can be omitted or assumed, because missing a 'not' can change the whole meaning of a passage. Consider the sentence below:

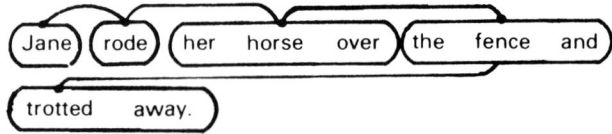

Here the fixations have been made over all the main points made in the sentence. The circles show the limit of each 'eye span' involved, so that when the reader fixes on horse, he also takes in 'her' and 'over' in the same eye span.

Notice that there is no fixed 'span'. It would not be sensible, for instance, to decide to fix on every fourth word. The range of each span depends very much on the material being read.

Eye span varies from person to person. Nobody should need to focus on every word, however. Eye span can be increased a small amount by practice. Concentrate on fixing less rather than on trying to stop pronunciation. By doing this and speeding up, you will be forced to stop subvocalising. If you try to concentrate on not pronouncing, however, you will become very confused!

Regression and visual wandering   Often regression (going back over material that has already been read) and visual wandering, can be the result of slow un-motivated reading practices. It is certainly true that if we read too slowly we become bored with what we are reading. This is partly because we have often forgotten what was written at the beginning of the sentence by the time we reach the end. Our eyes are not moving fast enough for our brains. As a result we do not take in the information the first time and are forced to go back and read it again. Regression then, can be caused by boredom and reading too slowly. Visual wandering is also, obviously, caused by boredom, not having to concentrate sufficiently on the material and therefore drifting off it. Regression, however, can also result from laziness. When we read normally we all know that we can go back and check a word whenever necessary and so our minds become lazy and we are forced to take in the information the first time.

Obviously we must get rid of unnecessary regression. The intelligent reader chooses when to regress. Sometimes it is necessary. For instance, when a new or difficult word is encountered, or where a passage or sentence appears in hindsight to have been of crucial importance, then it is justified. However, what is not justifiable is the habitual going back over words which are quite familiar.

To prevent this it is a good idea to practise reading with a card for a few days to prevent any going back at all. This will break the habit—then the card can be dispensed with.

How to use the card

The reader is here

Bring down the card at an angle exposing only the text to be read and covering the writing already looked at. Read *below* the card.

Practise this on your reading for the next few days; start now.

NB Your comprehension will suffer initially—persevere, it will be worth it in the end.

Reading faster— mental barriers

Just as we have all inherited mental barriers to not reading every word we see, we also developed in childhood the idea that 'reading slowly is reading well'. This is not true. We have already seen why this idea has developed in education and that there is no need for the stage which so often slows us down, the pronunciation stage. Reading faster often means reading more efficiently. Our minds are forced to concentrate harder if we read faster and do not allow ourselves to regress. There is no time for mental wandering. We also gain a certain impetus of gathering eye rhythm which helps us to read faster and also helps us to put together individual pieces of information into the whole picture which then emerges more clearly. Reading speeds of 1,000 words a minute are possible with comprehension of 70 per cent. This pre-supposes a *wish* to improve speeds and a *belief* that this can and should be done. Again, on a novel or work of art, it is perhaps not necessary or desirable to read quickly. Most of our reading problems boil down to lack of motivation to read faster. Do another exercise now, forcing yourself to read faster. You will find that, as with the regression exercise, your comprehension may suffer on the first few exercises because it will take a while for the mind to adjust to the new situation.

Concentration is a common problem. As we have seen above, this can often be cured by improving reading style. One can also do some practice, if this is a problem, at home every day. Just practise in order to concentrate on some reading for one minute. When you are sure that you are not wandering during this minute then extend it to two minutes and then three and so on. You will be very aware of when you have lost your concentration. Do not extend the time until you are sure of the previous one.

This is a simple but sure way of practising concentration and monitoring your improvement. Remember, concentration varies a lot depending on whether you are interested or not in the passage—use the same type of material for each practice.

Use a pencil or pen to direct your concentration. Many people feel that this is detrimental to reading, but in fact it can help the eyes to focus at the right point and prevent visual wandering. Do not move the head from side to side. The only problem arises when the pencil is moved too slowly, then obviously the reading suffers. It is possible, however, to use the pencil to push speeds faster. Do not try to use a pencil while you are still practising with the card! Practise reading fast, turning pages over quickly—reading the same exercise faster and faster. Try using a metronome for rhythm and speed.

Reading very fast in this way improves speed. Do not worry about comprehension while doing this. It is rather like driving along the motorway at 80 mph. Imagine having your speedometer covered over and being asked to slow down to 30 mph. You would do this, only to discover that you had actually slowed back to only 50 mph. You get used to travelling at a faster speed and then find the slower speeds 'too slow'. It is very similar in reading—speed up to 80 mph and when you go back to reading 'normally' you will find you are reading more quickly!

Physical problems There are other problems besides those of our own techniques. The ability of the writer and the situation in which we are reading also will have a considerable effect on our efficiency. We can allow for these things to a certain extent and this will be looked at when we consider the right approach to reading.

Summary The reader's eyes move in 'fixations' and 'saccades'. The major difference between a fast and slow reader is in the nature of the fixations:

1   Fix less often
2   Fix on groups of words and not single ones
3   Cut down fixation time by forcing yourself to read faster.

Remember, often a slow reader is an inefficient reader. Push your speed hard. It will seem to be an effort now, but you will naturally read faster after practice.

4 The right approach

Flexibility

Let us develop our approach to reading now in a wider field. It is not only necessary to be able to rapid read, but to adapt the style of reading to the circumstances. The essence of good reading is in flexibility. The average reader will read the newspaper at 250 words per minute, a letter from Aunt Mabel at the same speed and a report at work also. Flexibility must be applied in two ways:
- with each piece of material the type of reading to be employed can be decided beforehand—which approach is to be used
- within each piece of material the approach may have to be modified throughout according to changes in the material encountered.

What approach?

In rapid reading terms we talk of reading 'gears'. This is how we divide up the various approaches to reading into categories. These gears can be compared to the gears of a car. In a car, starting off in the right gear and changing gears regularly (being flexible) is very important—and so it is in reading. (Except that we are not restricted to starting in first gear every time)

The gears

What are the gears? There are four:
1 *Study reading.* Reading at a speed of up to 200 words per minute—can be as low as 50 words per minute. This is a technique of dealing with material and includes the other gears below. Hence it is the *equivalent* of reading at the above speed—it does not involve actually slowing the reading down to 50 words per minute; the same material is read more than once. Used when material is very difficult or 100 per cent comprehension is required. As with first gear in a car—it is a slow but high-powered gear.
2 *Slow reading.* This is the speed at which most people normally read everything. It ranges from about 200-300 words per minute. This gear is of very little use unless the material becomes a little difficult, as normally this is an inefficient speed. Generally, it is more efficient to read a piece twice very quickly than to read it once at this speed. Word by word, line by line progress. Except, of course, for novels, poems.
3 *Rapid reading.* This is your most useful gear. It is a speed of between 300-800 words per minute. It involves reading every word (but not fixing on every

one). It is used on material of average difficulty and would dictate a level of 60-70 per cent comprehension. This is sufficient for most everyday reading exercises. Line by line progress reading *groups* of words.

4 *Skimming.* The fastest gear. Speeds range from about 600 words per minute to 60,000 words per minute. Again, as with studying this is a speed *equivalent* to the above words per minute. With skimming, many of the words are not read at all as in reading. Words are missed out. The comprehension value of this exercise is much less than the other gears. It is most useful, however, for getting an overall idea of a passage, or finding specific information. It can be used most usefully in combination with the other gears.

So far we have looked at the difference between gears 2 and 3, efficient and inefficient reading. We will be examining gears 1 and 4 later.

What factors affect the style of reading?

There are three major areas affecting the way in which we should approach our reading, to guide us in our use of gears. As with driving a car, when we begin to learn gear changing we have to think about when it is necessary to use third or fourth gear. However, after a few weeks we are changing gear instinctively. As we approach a hazard we automatically change gear. So it is with reading. Changing speed becomes instinctive eventually, although it must be conscious at first. Compare the diagrams overleaf to see how similar rules apply in both cases.

The three factors which decide when we change gear, and indeed decide what gear we start out in when we read are:

(a) the nature of the material

(b) our purpose in reading

(c) external factors.

Let us consider each of these individually.

(a) *The material*

Several points need to be taken into consideration here. Difficulty is obviously one of the most apparent concerns for us. This could be related to *difficult concepts* involved or *difficult vocabulary*. (Or bad writing which will be dealt with in a moment.) Trying to appreciate difficult ideas or concepts in a passage should involve intense concentration and a combination of reading techniques. Reading through once, even very slowly is often not enough to appreciate this type of material, but a combination of skimming for the main

15

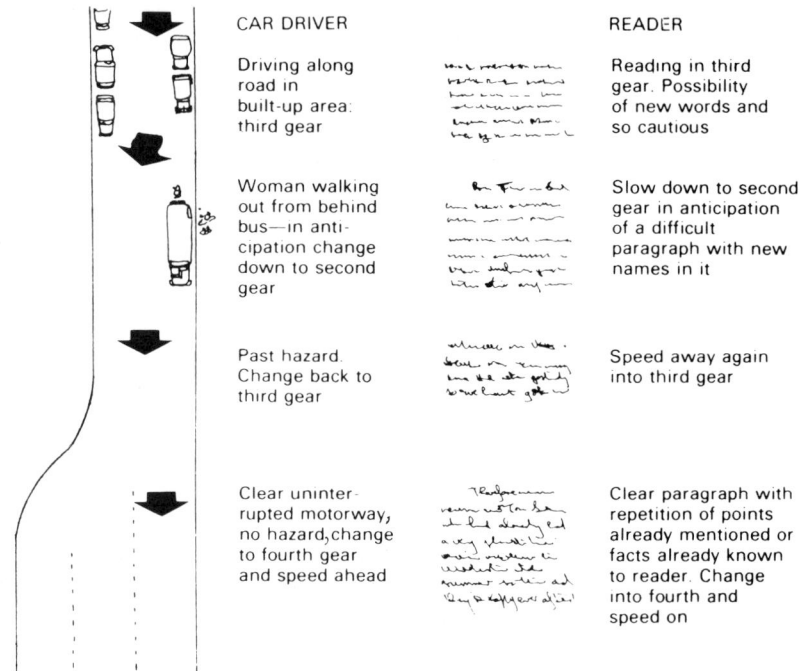

ideas, the whole idea and then rapid reading to fit each individual factor into the whole concept is the best way to tackle this. Or alternatively a study technique may be applicable for a very difficult piece.

On the other hand, if the problem is that of a *lack of vocabulary* or a poor vocabulary letting the reader down, then an effort can be made to improve this, although while it is still poor, obviously it will be necessary actually to stop and examine each unfamiliar word.

Prior knowledge of the subject matter is always a considerable advantage to the reader. Understanding and memory improve on a passage where some facts are easily recognisable. On material of this kind it is obviously most efficient to read a little faster.

Interest in the subject matter can be a considerable influence. An unmotivated reader is a poor reader. Do not slow down to try to make up for lack of interest. This will merely make the boredom more intense. Speed up and force yourself to concentrate harder, impose a discipline by testing yourself for knowledge of the content afterwards.

Badly written material is something that we can only suffer. The style of the author may be unnecessarily verbose, illogical or too brief to make any sense. The layout of the writing is also of great importance—a poor layout will slow reading down as much as a bad writing style.

(b) *Purpose*
Normally we know *why* we are reading, there is a reason. Making sure that we are aware of this before we begin to read is of prime importance. It helps us to be selective in our reading, but it also gives us a clue as to the style of reading with which it should be tackled. Sometimes we need to know the details of some material thoroughly. This may apply, for instance, to the reading of legislation. If we need *100 per cent comprehension* or need to memorise material, then we need to use a study technique, gear one. If, on the other hand, we want a *good understanding* of something but do not need to remember all the detail (perhaps with the reading of a report) then gear three, rapid reading, would be the most appropriate. Finally, if only a *vague outline,* a general idea of the main points, is required, then skimming is obviously adequate. This is often useful for reading documents before meetings, or getting the idea of a report before reading it in gear three. Being *selective* in our approach is a very important step towards efficient reading.

(c) *Other factors*
There are obviously other, external factors that are going to affect our style. We have to allow for these, although we can often do nothing about them.

Environment—the surroundings in which we decide or have to read, have a tremendous influence on us. Noise and constant *interruptions* are obviously fairly high on the list. If we have built up a good concentration level, however, noise around us can be largely eliminated by our minds with practice. It is perfectly possible to cut ourselves off from the rest of the world if our concentration is funneled down into one opening—our reading. This technique does not, however, get rid of interruptions such as the telephone and visitors. It is therefore necessary to consider whether it might not be a good idea to set aside reading 'periods' during the day when there are likely to be fewer interruptions. Some people, for instance, always read between 8.30 and 9.30 in the morning, because the office is quiet. Try taking lunch at a different time from most others, so that you can work peacefully while they are at lunch, or reading when most people have gone home at night. There is no easy answer.

The reader's state of mind. This is another factor to take into consideration. What time of day is it? Apart from the points mentioned above, we all have our own time clocks. This means that some of us concentrate more easily in the morning, others around midday, some in the afternoon, evening or early hours of the morning. Keep a diary for a week and note down the best times for working, and see at the end of the set period whether there is any correlation. This will give you a good clue as to when your reading would be most productive.

Relaxation is most important. Have a relaxed but alert mind and body. Having the right approach to reading will help to reduce tension when there is a time limit. Previously, with half an hour before a meeting and a 60-page document un-read in preparation, you may have panicked, started to read but been so worried knowing that you will not finish, that in fact you take in very little at all. Now looking at the problems objectively and putting together all the facts—you want to know as much as you can about the whole document—your restriction is that you only have 30 minutes in which to do it. In these circumstances, skimming in gear four would give the reader a fair knowledge of what the entire document contains. There may also be time then to go back to the odd sections of the document that you feel may be of particular interest and rapid read these for more detail. Using a method like this, far more will be derived from the material than would have been using the 'read-straight-through' method. Relax and deal with the material in the systematic way.

Relaxation is also a *physical* consideration. It is not a coincidence that typists are told to sit up with their backs straight and their feet on the floor, and that yoga advises the same basic position. In both cases the important point—whether sitting in a typist's chair or in the lotus position on the floor—is that the back should be at 90° to the floor. That is because this is the best position for all the senses to be functioning efficiently. The spinal column is straight and the blood circulation and messages from the nervous system can flow freely to the brain.

typist   lotus position

Holding the reading material directly in front of the eyes is a great help to our reading also. If the eyes are looking straight ahead, they are fully open and alert. If the book is held in the lap or on a desk then there is a greater tendency for the eyelids to close. Anyone who attempts to read lying down in bed will know that this is the best position in which to fall asleep!

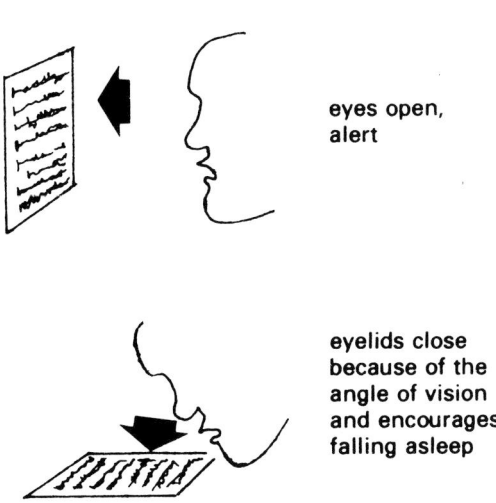

eyes open, alert

eyelids close because of the angle of vision and encourages falling asleep

In order to be truly flexible we have to take all of these three areas into account before we start to read, and be able to anticipate necessary changes in our style during the reading itself. The main points can be tabulated as follows:

Purpose	*Material*	*Other*
1 100% comprehension	1 Difficult ideas	1 Noise, interruptions
2 Memorise material	2 Difficult vocabulary	2 Time of day
3 Good understanding	3 Badly written/ laid out	3 Relaxation level (time limit)
4 General outline	4 Prior knowledge	4 Emotional barrier
5 Particular facts	5 Interest	5 Personal physical condition

Combination of gears

This choosing the right approach, like choosing the right gear in a car, becomes instinctive after a while. Often it is useful to combine gears to achieve the best results. Skimming can be used most usefully on almost any material as a preview to reading. It can also be used to review the material afterwards. We should not slow down reading speeds. If a preview has been done very rapidly, then the reading should be far faster. It is always more efficient to read something very quickly twice than it is to read it slowly once. Similarly rather than regress during the passage (breaking the rhythm) some readers prefer to mark, mentally, or with a pencil, the points that need to be checked again, and then these points may be reviewed together after the whole passage has been read. Try using these three techniques:

1 Preview then read
2 Preview read review
3 Read then review

Preview and review are both done by skimming—either before or after reading. Try not to allow this to slow your speed, practise until it is a speedy, efficient process. (See the section on skimming for clues on how to skim —page 28.)

Summary

The right approach involves flexibility of techniques. We must judge both our approach to material as a whole and be prepared to adapt this approach during the reading itself. The three major items that influence this approach are:

1 The material
2 The purpose in reading
3 External factors—in our surroundings
　　　　　　　　　　　　—within ourselves

A combination of the 'gears' is often the most efficient approach.

5 Understanding and remembering

Understanding

Having selected the parts that we need to concentrate on, we must achieve maximum understanding. Why is it sometimes easy to understand and at other times almost impossible? Well, a great many factors affect our understanding process. Some of these are:

The material
Difficulty of subject
Difficulty of language
Poor layout
Poor style

The environment
Interruptions
Distractions
Uncomfortable surroundings
Too comfortable surroundings

The reader
Lack of interest (or interest)
Physical fitness tiredness
Prior knowledge or lack of motivation
Feelings about the writer
Own views
Concentration level

We have come across these problems in a previous chapter—we can do little about the writing itself except adapt our reading style to allow for it. We can do a little about our environment, but the extent to which it affects our understanding does depend a great deal on our mental state. Therefore, we shall look primarily at the mental state of the reader and its affect on the reader's understanding. First, let us look at the process of understanding itself:

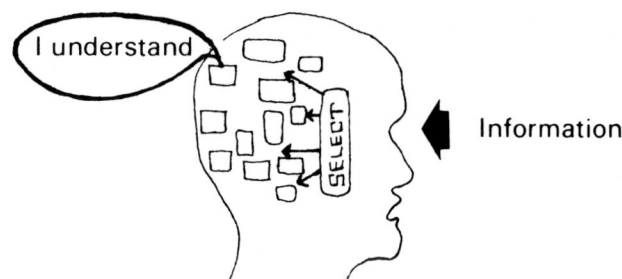

Information is received by the eyes and transmitted to the brain. Firstly it is divided into what is needed and not needed, then further divided into categories. These categories or 'frames of reference' are shown as squares

21

in the diagram. Similar information is stored together and understanding comes from the comparison of material within the category concerned. We understand by relating new information to similar material that we have already come across.

Let us look at how this process can be interrupted.

1 Lack of interest
   Physical fitness—tiredness } affect concentration
   Motivation

If the concentration is impaired by the factors above then the information will not even be selected, but discarded as not important enough at the select stage.

2 Lack of prior knowledge—can mean that the new information will be stored in a 'square' of its own. As there is no other information to relate to, there can be no 'understanding' only a recording of the fact. Here it is important to relate new material to any other material with which there is a connection so that it can be interpreted perhaps through another 'square's' contents.

3 Own views and feelings about the writer—the correct meaning is biased by our emotional reactions to the material or writer and therefore the understanding becomes distorted.

Our reading can be improved by adopting a *critical* approach. This will help the mind to organise material into appropriate categories for interpretation and in the process will involve the mind. Involvement breeds interest and concentration.

Rules for being critical

- consciously select material needed and not needed
- question material constantly:
    how does this relate to what I already know?
    what is the writer actually saying?
    is the writer saying what he means?
    do I agree with the writer?
    do the facts support the arguments?
    etc.
- try to build up a whole picture from the individual points:
    what are the main points?
    is there one important main point?
    what is the writer's objective?
    - to move from point to point towards a final conclusion
    - to write about a central argument/subject
    etc.

- summarise at the end in your mind to make sure you have the picture and the main points. If material is a page or more long, summarise material at regular intervals throughout as well as at the end.

Exercise

Do not worry about trying to do all of the above things at the same time. This may tie you in knots. It is important to work up to it in stages. Gradually all of these will be adopted until all are done at once. The mind is very capable of doing this.

1 Choose a passage and read slowly while questioning as suggested above
2 Using the same passage read through and summarise the content
3 Using the same passage, read through building up a picture as you go
4 Read through the passage: attempt to do all three.

Use this technique, practising on a different passage each day, at least once a day for the next week. When practising speed reading, forget this practice; eventually you will find that you will be doing this automatically while reading quickly. For the moment, practise them separately.

Memory

Memory is, as far as we know, based on several factors:
1 Getting the information selected into the frames of reference
2 Understanding
3 Putting in a strong enough memory 'trace' initially
4 Reinforcing information regularly.

So memory consists of:

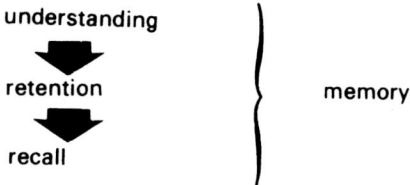

We have already dealt with understanding. It is absolutely necessary to understand before we can remember. Anyone who has attempted to memorise maths at school without understanding what the application is will know how difficult it is.

Retention

The facts need to be stored or retained before they can be referred to and used at a later date. Retention is a difficult area to test because we usually only know that we have retained if we can recall. However, if we do not remember it is not necessarily the case that we have failed on our retention—we may merely have failed to recall. But how often do we say 'I know that, but it has just slipped my mind'? We often remember the fact a few days later! So, it is possible to retain and not recall, but many failures in 'memory' occur because not enough trouble is taken in making sure that material is retained.

A 'memory trace' refers to material taken into the mind and the impact it has, as far as strength of memory is concerned. So, we can talk of a weak memory trace making little impact, and strong memory traces having a powerful impact.

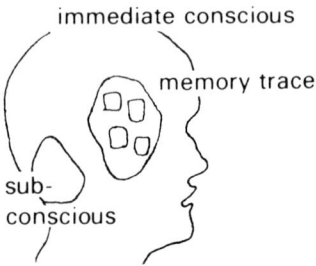

Immediate recall is normally only possible from the conscious mind. Information is stored in categories in the conscious for a limited period of time after which the memory trace fades. There is considerable evidence to show that it does not fade 'away' but goes into the sub-conscious. The information can no longer be immediately recalled at will (except under hypnosis).

The length of time that the information remains in the conscious depends on the original strength of the memory trace. If, for instance, a man daydreams while reading, then there will be a weak memory trace and it will fade very quickly. If he concentrates hard, however, then a strong memory trace which is longer lasting is produced. Unfortunately, even a strong memory trace will fade eventually. For normal purposes a single memory trace may be enough. However, for cases where longer lasting retention is needed, the important factor is reinforcement. It is most important to start reinforcing within the first three minutes after the first reading. Go over the points you want to remember. From then on, reinforcements can be further apart. Gradually build up the strength of the memory trace and you can remember for any length of time—but it is always necessary to remind yourself regularly—if only once a month!

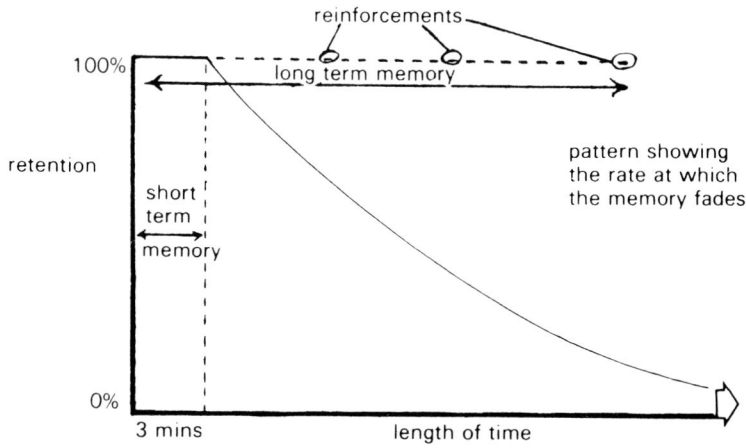

Recall

Once we have understood and retained the information we need, we can still fail at the recall stage. We know the information is there, what we now need is a foolproof way of being able to fish the information out at will. The two main ways are by using:
    association
    and labelling

Association

Not many people are born with 'good' memories; most successful memorisers have a 'system'. The basis of most of these systems is association. There are many ways of using this technique; it is most useful for remembering facts. Of course, many of us use these systems without being aware of it. For instance, how do you remember a telephone number? Look at the number below and decide *how* you are going to memorise it—do not just use a system of rote, this is generally inefficient.

684 9268

Ways of remembering by association
1 First set of numbers 8 is 2 more than 6 and the last number is 2 less than the first.
    Second set Then: the last two numbers are the same as the first two in the first set the first number is one more than the last and the only odd number, the second number is 2

Remembering the associations between the numbers helps us to remember the numbers. If you are not

25

mathematically minded, however, try some other versions:

2   The 68 bus goes to Grove Road
    The 92 bus goes to ???
    The 68 bus goes to ???
    4 is half the last number in the sequence.

OR

3   Woman with a fat waist   68-92-68
    Remember 4 as above.

ETC

There are many ways of remembering by association, only a few are shown above. Some methods are easier than others depending on the way your mind works most easily. Your method may not be shown—make one up; as long as there is a base of association memory will be more effective as a result.

Names of places or people can be dealt with in a similar way:

eg name of person—Duncan Wood—sounds like a Scottish tree
OR —Duncan is the forename of my uncle and I had a friend at school called (Denise) Wood

Remember the association and nudge your memory about the name!

Exercise

Go through the phone book picking out numbers and remembering them using your memory techniques. Go through a newspaper or magazine article and try to remember all the names of people and places and recall them afterwards (forget about speed for this exercise while practising). It is a good idea to read one of the books dealing with memory (see booklist in appendix 6). This will give you some examples of the many systems developed from the principle of association.

Labelling

This is a technique which helps us more to remember the context rather than the facts. It is extremely difficult to remember a string of points and it is inefficient to spend the time attempting to. So we can 'label' groups of associated points or happenings. Consider this example:

Remember the following letters and be able to repeat each one in order:

M E T H O D I S M
I S A N O N C O N
F O R M I S T R E
L I G I O N

It would be extremely difficult to read through the letters and remember them by rote. However, we may well make the job easier by grouping and labelling them:

methodism / is / a / non- / conformist / religion

Using this method we do not attempt to remember each letter—we remember six words instead of 33 letters. However, once the words are recalled, we know what letters make up each word, and so we can easily 'work out' the 33 letters.

Labelling works in a similar way. We recognise that a series of facts (or perhaps a paragraph of writing) have a common factor, eg they all relate to the legal aspect of the subject. We can, therefore, remember the label 'legal-aspect' and when we come back to produce the facts—the label reminds us of them under its heading.

Exercise Practise going through newspaper articles or a non-fiction book and labelling the main areas of the writing under headings and then remember these. Recall, using memorised headings.

NB Be careful to choose an appropriate 'label'. The wrong word can lead the memory off track and floor the memory entirely!

Summary In order to understand and remember we must:
1 Be selective
2 Get understanding by being critical:
    asking questions
    building a picture or structure
    summarising
3 Make sure of retention by:
    putting in a strong memory trace
    reinforcing the trace regularly
4 Make sure of recall by—using a system: association
    labelling

6 Skimming

Skimming can be the busy office worker's most valuable reading tool. When to use it:
1. When we want a general outline of the material (scanning/sampling)
2. When we only want certain information from a mass of material (locating)

Scanning and sampling

The easiest way to practise is on a newspaper.

Scanning— do not move the eyes rhythmically in blocks of words across the page as we do in reading. Allow the eyes to wander across the page without regular fixations. The eyes move where they want to, trying to pick out important words. Some people prefer to begin at the bottom of the page and move the eyes upwards —others, to move the eyes diagonally across the page—some move erratically all over the page. The important thing is *not* to have a line by line progress. It does not matter that parts are being missed —we are only after a general impression of the piece. Do it as quickly as you can. Take a newspaper article and get someone to mark how many words are in it. Give yourself a set time limit in which to skim it and begin. (Allow yourself a time limit of about one minute for 600 words.) Stop skimming when the minute is up and try to write down what you remember of the article. Keep practising in this way, gradually increasing the number of words to be covered in one minute.

NB Remember to *concentrate* as you scan, it is very easy to become mesmerised and merely move your eyes across the page without taking in anything.

Scanning: possible pattern of eye movement during scanning

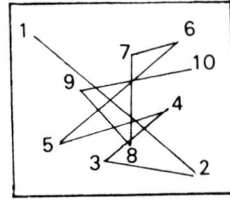

28

Sampling— is a different technique which achieves a similar result to scanning. When sampling, certain parts of the writing are chosen to be 'sampled' to give an outline picture of the whole. For instance, we may choose to read the introductory paragraph, the final paragraph and the first line of each paragraph. In a book we may choose to read the introduction, conclusion and look at all the chapter headings. This is a more structured way of achieving the same result as with scanning—a general outline. Test on a newspaper or magazine as with scanning—but decide before skimming which parts to read. Rapid read the parts to be sampled or, if confident, scan them well.

Sampling: possible pattern of eye movement during sampling

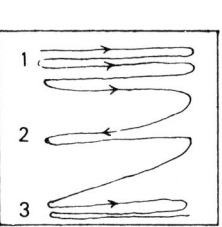

Examples of situations in which we might choose to scan or sample
1 In order to preview material before reading it
2 To review material after we have read it
3 To refresh our memories of the main points of some material that we are already familiar with or know about
4 To find out the bare outlines of a subject if we are pressed for time and cannot read the whole article (eg before a meeting)
5 To go through very easy or straightforward material
6 To get a general outline to increase our general knowledge of a subject without having to spend the time concentrating on it (eg trade magazines, newspapers, etc).

Locating

We all 'locate' whenever we use a telephone directory. If we want to find Mr K Jones we do not start at the beginning and work through until we find him—we calculate by deduction where his name will be. The mental process might be as follows:

1   We look for the J's
2   We look for 'Jo'
3   We look for 'Jon'
4   We find the 'Jones'
5   We look for 'K' initials
6   We find the 'K Jones'
7   We look for the right address
8   We find the name.

This process of mental deduction is also used for locating material in documents at work. If we require certain information from a document it is time wasting to read it all. We therefore use deduction to discover what we require. Using the index is essential if there is one, and noting the way in which the sections are headed. A good way to practise this method is to use legislation. Take an Act and ask a question about one of its provisions, then calculate where that information can be found before looking for it. Practise at becoming faster each time.

Examples of situations where we might locate:

1   To find details of legislation
2   To find parts of articles that are relevant to us
3   To extract information from a mass of material that we may need to use for a report.

Skimming is very fast—but has a poor capacity for comprehension and retention. It is extremely useful in combination with other methods to aid understanding, but poor on its own unless we need specific information or a general understanding. However, a great deal of material at work often falls into this category and could be 'polished off' very much more quickly using these methods.

Summary

Skimming does not involve reading every word, since when using this technique we purposely miss words and whole passages. It does not involve line by line progress or reading words in blocks.

7 Studying

The word 'studying' has probably conjured up all sorts of memories of schooldays and examinations. In fact, it is a word used to describe a systematic approach to any material that has to be understood fully or memorised. Some material cannot be rapid read—either because it is too difficult in its content, or because more than 70 per cent comprehension is required. The secret to successful studying lies in having a good system of approach. Merely reading the material over three or four times is not sufficient and certainly not very efficient. The most popular study systems use a logical approach to the problem by tackling the material in a way in which the mind will find it most easy to assimilate it. One of the most widely used systems is: *SQ3R* One of the most popular methods. It involves:

S— Survey the material. Skim through it to get the gist—an idea of the 'whole' to fit the parts into.

Q—Question. Decide what questions need to be answered by the material (encouraging the mind to be discriminating).

R—Read the material at whatever speed you are able—normal rapid reading.

R—Recite—that is take notes by going back over the important points. Take *only* key notes to jog the memory later.

R—Revise the notes (not the original material). This is most important—remember the section on long-term memory—it is necessary to revise regularly, particularly at first—in order to strengthen the memory. Revising the original is a waste of time if you have good key notes.

Summary   Studying, or gear one, should be used when the material is difficult; when more than 70 per cent comprehension is needed or when it is necessary to learn the material. The most effective way is to adopt a system of approach which works for you personally.

8 Final summary

Reading well is a question of being flexible and adopting the right approach to material.

1. Firstly, get rid of bad habits which will prevent you from reading quickly when the material allows it. Do not worry about pronouncing every word —concentrate on recognising the 'symbol' and read for the *meaning* of the passage. This will allow you to read across the page in 'blocks' of several words taken in by one eye span. (Remember—do not attempt to miss words.) Speed up even more by preventing unnecessary regression. This will enable you to rapid read. Do not worry too much about comprehension while developing this skill—develop speed and then worry about understanding later. Once you are reading quickly enough you will find that you have automatically stopped subvocalising because it is not possible at very high speeds.

2. Use the best approach for the purpose and type of material—use the right gears.

3. Remember to be critical when reading—question and summarise the material while reading it in order to comprehend properly. Memory involves:
    understanding
    retaining
    recalling
   Put in a strong memory trace and use the techniques of association and labelling—trigger and 'key' words to memorise material. *Remember* a good memory is *developed* using systems, it is not necessary to be born with a photographic memory.

4. Skim when a general outline is needed or when specific information needs to be extracted. Use either scanning, sampling or locating but do not read in blocks or make line by line progress. Study where material is difficult or good comprehension or memory is required. Again, use a systematic approach—be efficient.

Once you are reading faster and better—read *more*. Most of us only read what we have to get through at work saying that there is no time for anything apart from this. Often this is an excuse because an inefficient reader gets through a book so slowly that he appears never to get through the whole work! It is important to read as much and as widely as possible to improve reading skills. Why?

Good, fast reading is based on the reader being able to recognise words (symbols) and interpret them very quickly. It follows that the more familiar the reader is with the words the more easily and quickly he will be able to interpret them. *Any* reading material includes words and so anything will do—although the more widely you read, the less often you will come across an unfamiliar symbol.

The more you read, the more you will want to read, the more interesting different subjects become. Those of you who are sceptical—try it and practise your reading in the process.

The best of luck—and keep at it!

APPENDIX 1 **Reading test 1**

Instructions Test your starting speed on the following exercise. Use a watch with a second hand. Check time of starting and begin to read. Check finishing time. Write down in minutes and seconds the length of time taken to read the passage.
- answer the test questions
- look up the answers on page 42 and mark the result. Start now . . .

The Pyramid Effect
The pyramids on the west bank of the Nile were built by the pharaohs as royal tombs and date from about 3000 B C. The most celebrated are those at Giza, built during the fourth dynasty, of which the largest is the one that housed the pharaoh Khufu, better known as Cheops. This is now called the Great Pyramid. Some years ago it was visited by a Frenchman named Bovis, who took refuge from the midday sun in the pharaoh's chamber, which is situated in the center of the pyramid, exactly one third of the way up from the base. He found it unusually humid there, but what really surprised him were the garbage cans that contained, among the usual tourist litter, the bodies of a cat and some small desert animals that had wandered into the pyramid and died there. Despite the humidity, none of them had decayed but just dried out like mummies. He began to wonder whether the pharaohs had really been so carefully embalmed by their subjects after all, or whether there was something about the pyramids themselves that preserved bodies in a mummified condition.

Bovis made an accurate model of the Cheops pyramid and placed it, like the original, with the base lines facing precisely north-south and east-west. Inside the model, one third of the way up, he put a dead cat. It became mummified, and he concluded that the pyramid promoted rapid dehydration. Reports of this discovery attracted the attention of Karel Drbal, a radio engineer in Prague, who repeated the experiment with several dead animals and concluded, 'There is a relation between the shape of the space inside the pyramid and the physical, chemical, and biological processes going on inside that space. By using suitable forms and shapes, we should be able to make processes occur faster or delay them'.

Drbal remembered an old superstition which claimed that a razor left in the light of the moon became blunted. He tried putting one under his pyramid, but nothing happened, so he went on shaving with it until it was blunt, and then put it back in the pyramid. It became sharp again. Getting a good razor blade is still difficult in many Eastern European countries, so Drbal tried to patent and market his discovery. The patent office in Prague refused to consider it until their chief scientist had tried building a model himself and found that it worked. So the Cheops Pyramid Razor Blade Sharpener was registered in 1959 under the Czechoslovakian Republic Patent No. 91304, and a factory soon began to turn out miniature cardboard pyramids. Today they make them in styrofoam.

There is a fascinating postscript to this pyramid story. In 1968 a team of scientists from the United States and from Ein Shams University in Cairo began a million-dollar project to X-ray the pyramid of Chephren, successor to Cheops. They hoped to find new vaults hidden in the six million tons of stone by placing detectors in a chamber at its base and measuring the amount of cosmic-ray penetration, the theory being that more rays would come through hollow areas. The recorders ran twenty-four hours a day for more than a year until, in early 1969, the latest, IBM 1130, computer was delivered to the university for analysis of the tapes. Six months later the scientists had to admit defeat: the pyramid made no sense at all. Tapes recorded with the same equipment from the same point on successive days showed totally different cosmic-ray patterns. The leader of the project, Amr Gohed, in an interview afterward said, 'This is scientifically impossible. Call it what you will—occultism, the curse of the pharaohs, sorcery, or magic, there is some force that defies the laws of science at work in the pyramid.'

(543 words)

Questions

1 What was it about the animals that had wandered into the Great Pyramid that caught the Frenchman Bovis' attention?
2 Describe the experiment Bovis did to test his theory about the pyramid.
3 Describe Drbal's experiments with razors.
4 Describe the reaction of the Czechoslovakian Patent Office to Drbal's patent application.
5 What are Drbal's pyramids made of today?
6 In what direction must a test pyramid be orientated?
7 From where came the team of scientists who did X-ray studies of the pyramid of Chephren?
8 What did their studies reveal?
9 Where is the most celebrated pyramid?
10 Describe conditions inside the Great Pyramid.

Answers: see page 42.

Now, you should have a time written down and a mark out of ten for comprehension of the passage.

Change the time into words per minute—look up the table in Appendix 3. Look down the left-hand column for your time and across the top line for the number of words in the passage. Read across from the left and down from the top. The figure where they meet is your words per minute score.

Example:
If it had taken you 3 minutes 5 seconds, look down the left-hand column for 3 min 5 sec and across the top for the nearest number to 543 (number of words in the passage). This gives you a score of 178 words per minute.

Now change your comprehension score into a percentage (multiply by 10) so that 6 out of 10 = 60 per cent.

you now have two scores—words per minute (speed)
—comprehension (percentage)

Keep a record of these, they represent your present speed and comprehension.

Reading test 2

Use this exercise as your final test to compare with the initial one.

Krakatau's turbulent child echoes cataclysm
The Child of Krakatau is growing restive. For the past two weeks, the island volcano has been trembling in the manner of its infamous parent, spewing columns of fire and ash and sending shock waves through the Sunda Strait between Java and Sumatra.

Stepping onto this nightmare landscape of black ash and lava, one is reminded uncomfortably of the cataclysmic explosion that shook the world on August 26, 1883, when Krakatau erupted with the biggest bang in recorded history.

More than 36,000 people died when *tsunamis* (tidal waves) up to 135ft high swept through the straight at 350 mph and devestated hundreds of coastal villages and towns. The waves were registered in the English Channel, and a giant dust cloud circling the earth created optical illusions and altered the climate of the northern hemisphere for several years.

Sudanese natives blamed the Dutch colonial authorities for failing to offer blood sacrifices to volcano spirits and sea ghosts prowling the area.

From its *caldera* (collapsed crater) 200 metres beneath the sea, Krakatau gave birth to four islands early this century, but only one survived the pounding surf. Anak (child of) Krakatau, which emerged in 1930, is now some 600ft high and growing steadily with the violence of its progenitor.

An intermittent series of eruptions died down in 1981, allowing it to become a tourist attraction, but it began stirring from its slumber again late last month. During such periods of activity, Indonesian officials urge visitors to view events from the safety of their hotels on the coast of west Java, 30 miles away.

This sensible advice is occasionally ignored by small groups of the brave or foolhardy who charter fishing boats for 10-hour round-trips from Dr Axel Ridder, manager of the Carita Krakatau Beach Hotel. Dr Ridder, an erstwhile West German government employee, doctor of philosophy and raconteur, likes to shock his clients by informing them they have an 80 per cent chance of coming back.

'They are totally crazy, *ja!*' he observes cheerfully. 'The professors say you can't predict anything, but we promise to give them certificates and they go away.' Dr Ridder hasn't lost anyone yet, but there have been mishaps. In 1986, two American women were reduced to living on rainwater and toothpaste when the engine of their boat failed, and they drifted for three weeks.

A few years earlier, Dr Ridder was standing on an outer ridge of the volcano when it erupted without warning. 'You saw everywhere fire-balls, and boulders were falling all around me. I couldn't take photographs because my hands were shaking so, and I started to run. I should be dead already.'

Local experts are not unduly concerned by the volcano's adolescent tantrums, believing it to be a safe distance from inhabited regions. But that's what the Dutch colonial authorities thought in 1883.

Questions

1 What is the name of the volcano featured in the article?
2 What and when was 'the biggest bang in recorded history?'.
3 Name at least one worldwide effect of this biggest bang.
4 In what way does tour operator Dr Ridder shock his clients?
5 What is a tsunami? A caldera?
6 What did the American women adrift at sea eat?
7 How many tourists have been killed on the island this year?
8 On what did the Sudanese natives blame the eruption?
9 What one word is used to sum up Krakatan's child?

Answers: see page 42.

10 What overall impression have you gained of volcanic activity in the area?

Note the time taken and your mark out of ten for comprehension. Calculate the words per minute from Appendix 3 and change the mark out of ten into a percentage.

38

APPENDIX 2 **Marking chart**

'A' Comprehension

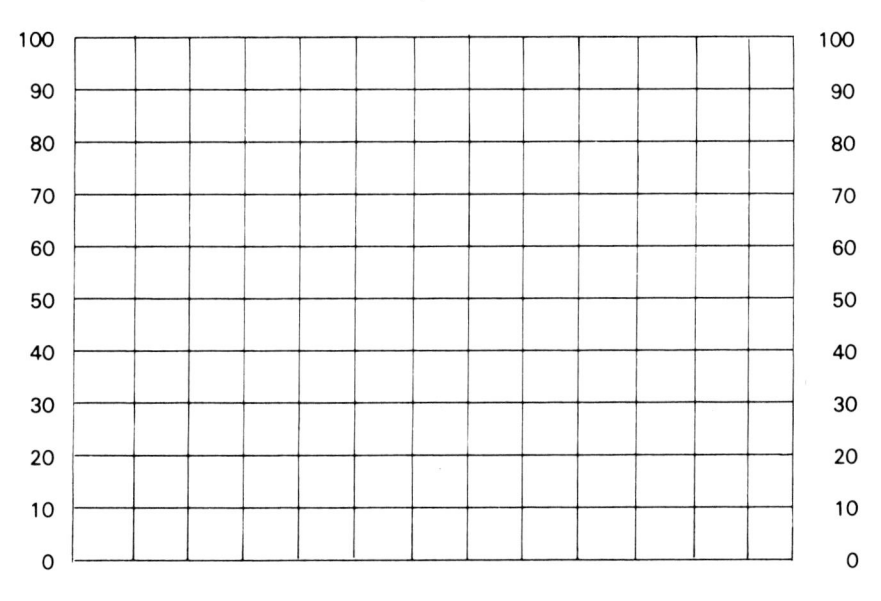

'B' Speed

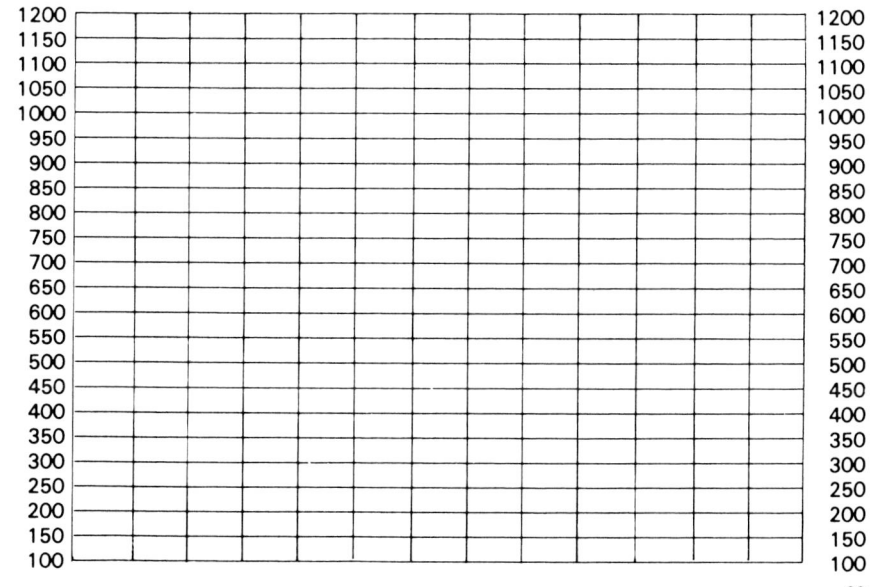

APPENDIX 3 Reading speed conversion table

Time Taken	400	500	600	700	800	900	1000	1100	1200	1300	1400	1500	1600	Time Taken
0.30	800	1000	1200	1400	1600	1800	2000	2200	2400	2600	2800	3000	3200	0.30
0.35	685	857	1030	1200	1370	1560	1734	1884	2055	2230	2400	2562	2740	0.35
0.40	600	750	900	1050	1200	1360	1510	1648	1800	1960	2100	2250	2400	0.40
0.45	533	668	800	934	1066	1200	1334	1456	1599	1740	1860	2004	2132	0.45
0.50	480	600	720	840	960	1090	1206	1314	1440	1560	1680	1800	1920	0.50
0.55	436	545	660	764	872	988	1096	1207	1308	1420	1520	1638	1744	0.55
1.00	**400**	**500**	**600**	**700**	**800**	**900**	**1000**	**1100**	**1200**	**1300**	**1400**	**1500**	**1600**	**1.00**
1.05	369	461	558	646	746	840	934	1021	1107	1200	1292	1383	1492	1.05
1.10	343	427	525	600	693	780	867	942	1029	1120	1200	1281	1386	1.10
1.15	320	401	483	560	640	720	800	883	960	1040	1120	1203	1280	1.15
1.20	300	375	450	525	604	680	755	824	900	980	1050	1125	1208	1.20
1.25	282	354	425	494	569	640	711	776	846	920	988	1062	1138	1.25
1.30	267	334	400	467	534	600	667	728	800	870	930	1002	1068	1.30
1.35	250	317	380	442	509	573	635	694	750	820	884	951	1018	1.35
1.40	240	300	360	420	483	545	603	660	720	780	840	900	966	1.40
1.45	228	286	344	400	457	517	571	630	684	740	800	858	914	1.45
1.50	218	273	328	382	436	494	548	600	655	710	760	819	872	1.50
1.55	209	261	314	365	419	472	524	575	627	680	730	783	838	1.55
2.00	**200**	**250**	**300**	**350**	**400**	**450**	**500**	**550**	**600**	**650**	**700**	**750**	**800**	**2.00**
2.05	192	240	288	336	384	431	481	528	577	625	675	719	768	2.05
2.10	184	231	276	323	368	413	462	506	554	600	650	693	736	2.10
2.15	177	223	267	311	355	396	445	489	534	580	625	669	710	2.15
2.20	171	215	258	300	342	380	428	472	514	560	600	645	684	2.20
2.25	165	208	249	290	331	370	414	456	497	540	580	622	662	2.25
2.30	160	200	240	280	320	360	400	440	480	520	560	600	640	2.30
2.35	155	194	232	271	310	349	387	426	465	505	545	583	620	2.35

2.40	150	188	225	262	300	339	374	412	450	490	530	564	600	2.40
2.45	146	181	217	255	293	329	363	398	437	475	513	543	586	2.45
2.50	143	174	209	247	286	319	352	384	424	460	495	522	572	2.50
2.55	138	170	204	240	276	309	342	376	412	447	480	511	552	2.55
3.00	**133**	**167**	**200**	**233**	**266**	**300**	**333**	**368**	**400**	**435**	**465**	**501**	**532**	**3.00**
3.10	126	158	190	221	253	285	316	348	379	410	440	474	506	3.10
3.20	120	150	180	210	240	269	300	330	360	390	420	450	480	3.20
3.30	114	143	171	200	229	258	286	314	343	370	400	429	458	3.30
3.40	109	137	164	191	219	247	272	300	327	355	380	411	436	3.40
3.50	104	131	157	182	209	236	260	288	313	340	365	393	418	3.50
4.00	**100**	**125**	**150**	**175**	**200**	**225**	**250**	**275**	**300**	**325**	**350**	**375**	**400**	**4.00**
4.10		119	145	166	191	214	240	263	287	310	335	357	382	4.10
4.20		113	136	157	182	203	230	251	274	295	320	339	364	4.20
4.30		110	133	153	177	198	222	244	267	290	312	334	355	4.30
4.40		107	129	150	171	190	214	236	257	280	300	322	342	4.40
4.50		104	124	145	165	185	207	228	248	270	290	311	331	4.50
5.00	**80**	**100**	**120**	**140**	**160**	**180**	**200**	**220**	**240**	**260**	**280**	**300**	**320**	**5.00**
5.30			108	127	146	164	181	200	218	237	256	271	293	5.30
6.00			100	116	133	150	166	184	200	217	232	250	266	6.00
6.30				108	124	139	155	165	185	201	216	232	248	6.30
7.00				100	114	129	143	157	171	185	200	214	229	7.00
7.30					107	120	134	142	160	174	187	200	214	7.30
8.00					100	112	125	137	150	162	175	187	200	8.00
8.30						106	118	129	141	153	165	177	188	8.30
9.00						100	111	122	133	144	155	166	177	9.00
9.30							105	116	127	137	147	158	168	9.30
10.00							100	110	120	130	140	150	160	10.00
11.00								100	109	118	128	135	146	11.00
12.00									100	108	116	125	133	12.00
13.00										100	108	116	124	13.00
14.00											100	107	114	14.00

APPENDIX 4 Answers to reading tests

1 The Pyramid effect
1 They had not decayed but were mummified.
2 He made a scale model of the pyramid and placed a dead cat inside, one third of the way up. It became mummified.
3 A sharp razor placed one third of the way up inside a model pyramid did not become dull, but a dull razor placed there became sharp again.
4 They refused his application until their Chief Scientist tried it himself and found it worked. They then granted him a patent.
5 Styrofoam.
6 With base lines facing magnetic north-south and east-west.
7 From the United States and Egypt.
8 The data made no sense at all. 'There is some force that defies the laws of science at work in the pyramid.'
9 Giza.
10 The inside of the Great Pyramid was unusually humid.

2 Krakatau's turbulent child echoes cataclysm
1 Anak Krakatau
2 Krakatau eruption, 1883
3 Air pollution, waves, climate
4 80 per cent chance of returning
5 Tidal wave, collapsed crater
6 Toothpaste
7 None
8 They blamed the Dutch authorities for failing to offer sacrifices to the volcano and the sea.
9 Turbulent
10 Very active; on-going; brings tourists to the area; at a safe distance from inhabited regions.

APPENDIX 5 **How to test yourself**

Practise your reading whenever you can. Any piece of writing will do. However, try to choose material of similar difficulty so that your graph will represent a real increase. A harder text will obviously cause you to score lower, and vice versa. It is best to:

1 choose a book—and work through that; OR
2 always test yourself on the same newspaper
- read a passage, time yourself and record the time
- count the number of words in the passage after you have read it
- work out the two scores—words per minute and comprehension

Test yourself at least once a day, the more you practise the better you will become.

APPENDIX 6 **Further reading**

Read better, read faster, M and E De Leeuw, Pelican
Reading faster: a drill book, E Fry, Cambridge University Press
Efficient reading, C Mares, Teach Yourself Books
Towards efficiency in reading, G R Wainwright, Cambridge University Press
Read well and remember, O Webster, Pan
Rapid reading, G R Wainwright, W H Allen
Use your head, T Buzan, BBC Publications